Blue Pollen Beautiful

Elizabeth Goodsir
& Madeleine Goodwolf

Blue Pollen Beautiful

Acknowledgements

With love and appreciation to Bruce Goodsir –
husband and father of the book-makers.
His artist's eye and lover's heart have scanned each
and every line with deep knowing.

And special thanks to Terry Whitebeach for supporting
me during my late arrival to the world of writers; and for
endorsing this book with such unconditional generosity.
She blessed this book, not as an editor, but as co-woman,
co-mother, co-elder.

Blue Pollen Beautiful
ISBN 978 1 76041 261 6
Copyright © text Elizabeth Goodsir 2016
Copyright © images Madeleine Goodwolf

First published 2016 by
GINNINDERRA PRESS
PO Box 3461 Port Adelaide 5015 Australia
www.ginninderrapress.com.au

Blue Pollen Beautiful was shortlisted in the 2015 Tasmanian Premier's Literary Prizes.

It received an award for the University of Tasmania Prize for unpublished works.

It won the People's Choice for the University of Tasmania Prize, 2015.

a mother writes
her daughter draws

my daughter was busy cleaning out her studio
discarding all her early etchings

I couldn't let the quaint   quirky   clever drawings
disappear without being shared one more time

it led me to look at my own early writing
simple curious lines of wandering and wondering

images and words playing with what it is to be human
they asked to be put together

Life

you're so beautiful

couldn't be more roly-polying
grassy hopper
more berry rasping
cone pining
bee bumbling
sky larky

so soul lifty

The starlings

are busy
singing
strutting
swapping places

they peck
and gather
fill the trees
crazy with laughter

a fresh morning's
a gamble
a gift
they giggle

dropping from
bent branches
into wild
wet wind

Lovers don't finally meet somewhere
they've been in each other all along

I was lucky my mother
stayed in her mind
and body

she had maps to live by
and gave me time
to trace them
to plot my own
notice the contours
join the dots

I lay my line
over hers
and notice
how many times
we reach the same
points of elevation

It has been said

as people get older
they get more alike
and could be leading
the same life

but what about the man
who smiled…life's but a joke
and his wife
who insisted…life is no joke

in the same room
walking circles

in opposite directions

Sometimes we need
to taste a giraffe
a bird
a flower
not just know about them

I'm smiling

simply
because
I believe
in miracles

When I became mother
something happened
between my mother and
her mother

and I could hear it between
my mother and me
and now between
my daughter and me

what is it I hear
as I watch her
transform in the eyes
of her new born

the shuffle of women
making more space

I wonder where   when
I learned to be other

someone I supposed
believed was expected

imagined there was a
right me to become

isn't it time I trusted
floating on the tide

even if now and again
it's bottled

My classmate

says she doesn't write poems
she scribes others' stories
edits and corrects manuscripts
she is paid for her skill

there is a right way of doing it

I hide my pages of short sentences
spilling my secrets and cravings
clumsy ways of saying what I love
stack them in a fruit box under my shoes

they have no right

I rode my life today
like a charioteer

tall and straight
and brave

breath was all it took

any instant can take it

Our love is
not a tug of war

rather…
we are sea-grasses
borne up by each wave
as it passes
drawn down by each wave
that recedes

anchored
lucid

A writer mother reminded me

I am the boat that sailed you
I pulled you into your skin
bound you to your bones

finished and complete
I took you to the shore
and gave you to eternity

Dusk

it's the moment when the house
shrinks and reshapes

the light-filled shell alive with
sunshine and shadows

turns cave-like
rich with rugs and downy cushions

candle wax and deep sound
no drapes screen the growing darkness

the moon stands bare
ready to dance through strips of glass

onto silver spoons and red wine
wear itself in our hair

decide to stay in our tabernacle
whilst the sky moves on

Australia Day

four dandelions open
small suns on green lawn
our new emblem?

Sorry Day

I'm Aboriginal   she said
her eyes shining from
her pale freckled face

I'm sorry   I said
and bowed my head
in thanks

I like telling you
she gifted softly
we watched our hands

clasp across the counter
lifting her head she spoke
for the queue to hear –

I wish they were black

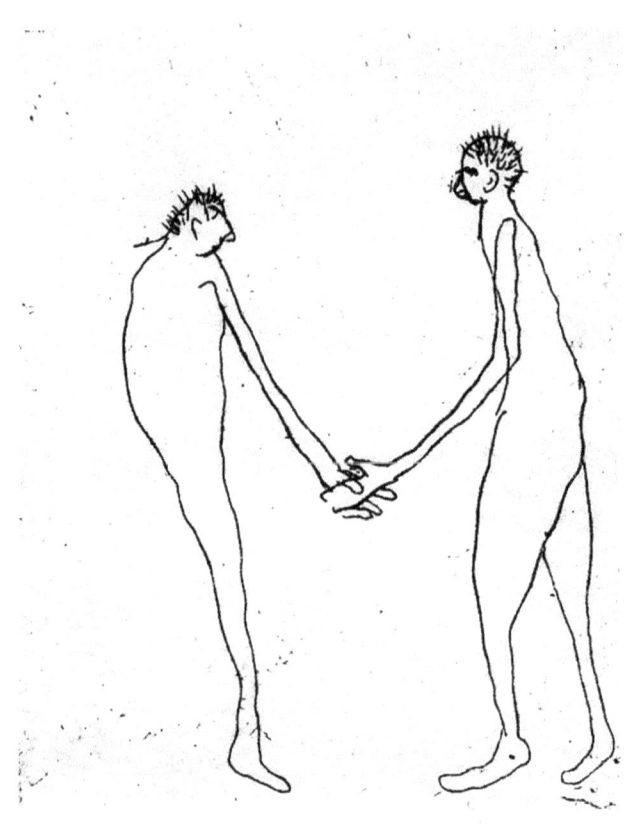

My guide

takes me to strange
and awkward places
but with firm
warm hands
that I trust
as soon as I let go
of my hold on myself

It has been a fierce
midsummer
all ablaze or aflood

swaths of island
wilderness
burnt to ashes

old growth forest
expired in the
intensity of its own fire

verdant valleys rich farmland
awash with flooding rivers
tumbling run-off

the rest is still
quiet   sad
with haze or debris

in the cool and the calm
of mellow days
how haunted we will be

with the failure
to notice
to treasure this earth

Coming home

he comes home
with nothing to say
it's clear though
that something's wrong
he lies down fully dressed
shuts out the world with a pillow

he's mid-life
but not at the moment
for now
he's back in his mother's womb
tomorrow he'll explain his clever scheme
to successful clients

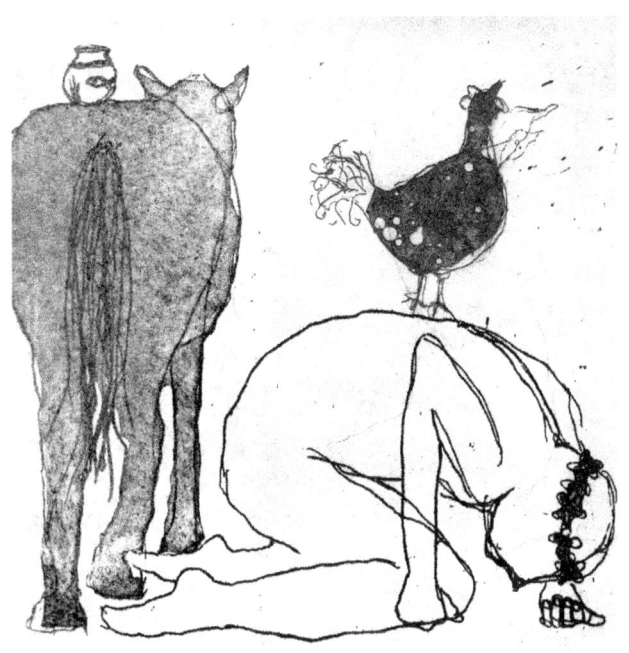

Some people talk of living with a heavy coat
find it hard to breathe
to move

I prefer to feel the cold in
my own light clothes
think how warm I used to be

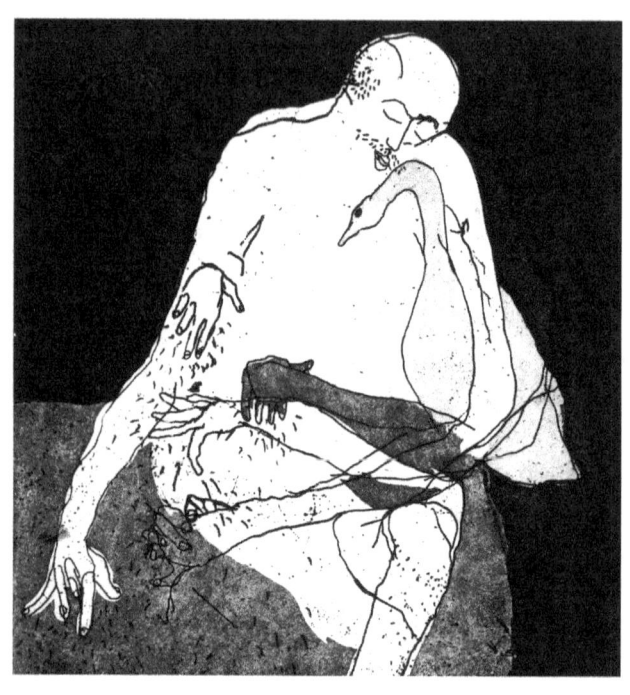

The bay a silver shimmer
the days serene
and grey

wish this into every corner
of our tired
brave earth

Walking a
breathlessly
still beach
two rainbows
threw themselves
from the golden point
and landed all
colours flaring
into the sea

seconds before
moody clouds
swooped
surrounded
suffocated

In the purplish greyness
a white sail
heaved a lumpy river
down to the sea

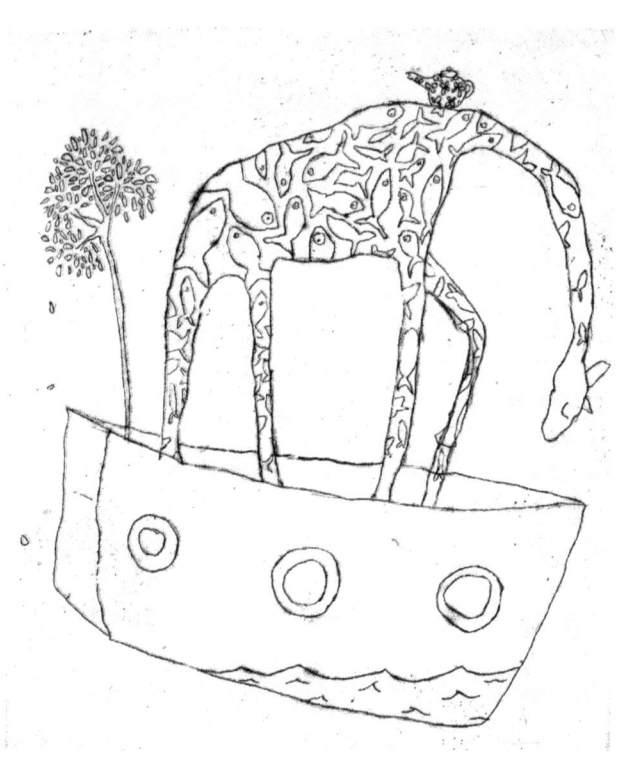

Beauty

whiteshell   turquoise
abalone beautiful
jet beautiful
fool's gold beautiful
blue pollen beautiful

Turning Point

it seems this is the time to wonder
where had I arrived
and what I came to be

which thought or deed
has been true
where had I strayed   resisted

what stranger helped me touch them
springing child-like kindness
from my untapped wells

the ants that
made me rethink
the tree that pierced such ingratitude

it seems this is the time to
keep
turning

The day as dry

as a splinter
sky congested with
teasing clouds

the river
green
not with rain

but with ash
from the
burning north

the night a pregnant wait

Equinox

lying in white-curtain light
still as heat drunk
gum leaves
in our summer
sea shell

until the violet sea
insists we run the
beach
dive away
our salty night

We laugh at the
reflecting water
for rippling our faces

even more than what
had taken the sun to do
for seventy years

Immuned

they had walked through a door
they didn't mean to
stayed there like frogs
in rising temperatures

Less

strange how we don't mind
an upturned beetle

struggling on the path

all stays the same
the sky is blue

we continue our walk

it's part of nature
they don't feel

nothing much has happened

they know their place
don't expect   demand   haunt

that's reserved for us

My home fits me
like a nutshell
matches my shape
and opens when
I'm ready

Once bearded
balding
grey curls at his neck
furrowed features
and thought-filled forehead
hands ink-stained or with garden dirt

now

see him reading
stand up
straighten his woollen vest
move slowly towards the door
offering   waiting
see him stay here just for her

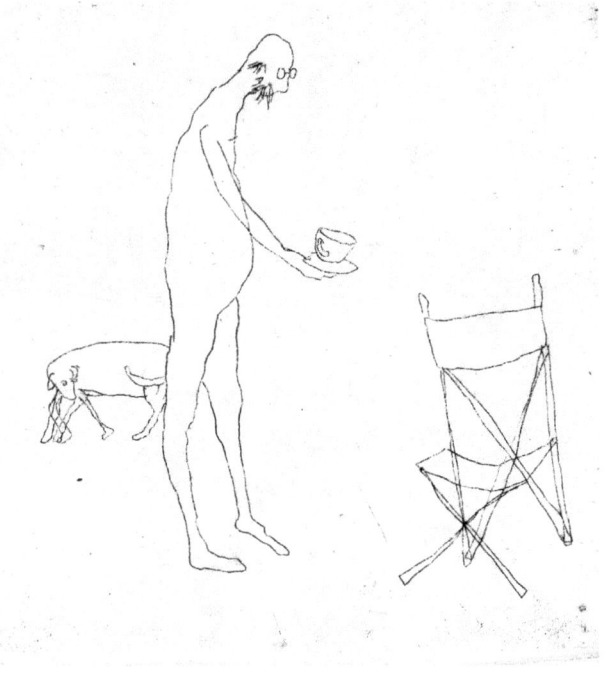

Two precious friends had shared time
one listening   guiding   making safe

on departing the other spoke of her
disappointment

the sharing had not been really fruitful
perhaps it takes courage to shake the tree

Landscape

I am the woman under the tree
see the yellow skirt
flowered straw hat
see how I carry the laden plate
slowly so not to walk out of the frame

if you call her now I wonder would she hear you
and if she did
could she find you
but you will know her by the impossible gestures
the meandering of her mad   glad stories

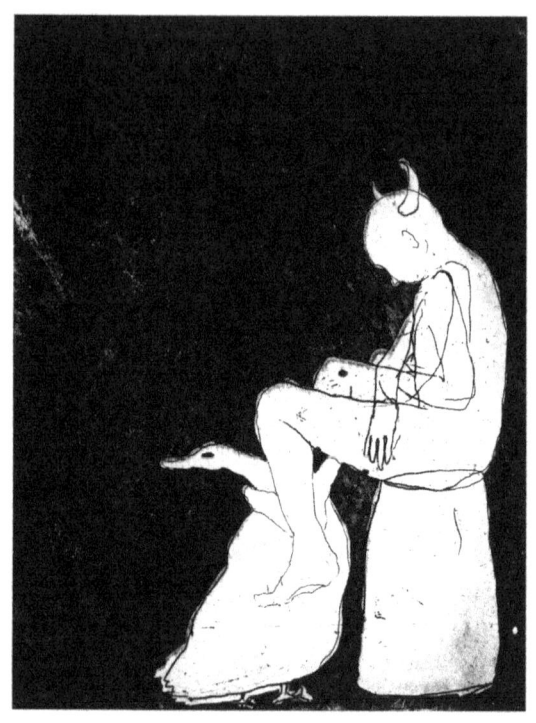

In loneliness and need
grabbing
claiming
inventing greed

stealing freedom
envying love
forgetting peace
beyond   above

we are deeply
searching for
letting go
letting be

Behind the seen

I went a whole day not
knowing what I was doing
where I was going
who I met   talked to

the sun flared and died
earth rotated
I breathed
ate   walked

someone would have seen me
in such-and-such colour
heard my steps
noticed if I was home

thought I was busy
preoccupied
I was
I was hiding out with you

like I have to now
in the only place left
somewhere behind
my eyelids

People are in the streets marching
shouting their minds

do I join
afraid of apathy

or stay behind my door
frightening myself

Divided Hemispheres

from a summer
playground

the sun blew
out of site

a red ball tossed
over the horizon

perhaps landing
cracking   breaking

exploding   whole
families apart

village after
village asunder

If I were a curlew

I'd travel for days across
stubble grass and dunes

under shooting stars
and a sling of light in a velvet sky

and my song would be as soft
as the cries of a stolen land

At last

I wear clothes like pages torn from a book
leave the dirt grey as bone under my nails

have hair of dead leaves
thin driftwood wrists

engraved and inked skin
thinner than whispers

roots for feet
wander each gone day

a wind dances me to the edge
and my song is of no reason

Of course

only a woman would
dream a fish to fly
a platypus that
feeds its chicks on milk
furry animals with fingered hands

because we can't say no

I had dreaded this moment
of meeting
after our last words

but we smiled
and you passed
like wind going

over my
outstretched
hand

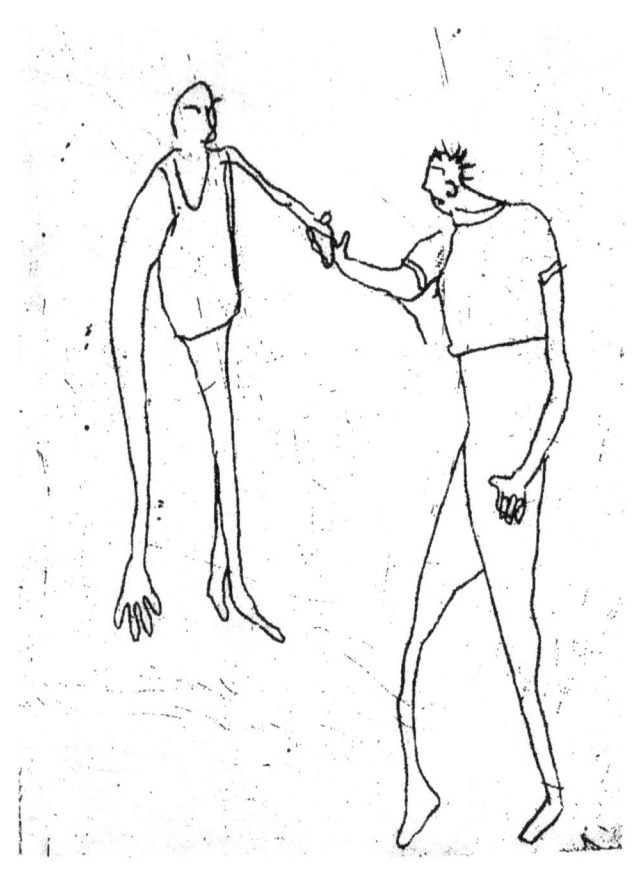

He wanted to say
you ought not to trust me
why not
someone would ask
because I'm a stranger to myself
he needed to hear out loud

My neighbour stands
like a blade of grass
beneath the wind

soon
like the wind
she will be gone

for now her
laughter still
bursts like

a silver balloon
onto red geraniums
yellow tea cups

it will hang
in the she-oaks
on each curl of the sea

And there is a time
when the searching
the swinging
the leaping
and the falling
lead us to
receiving

They walked
side by side
silent

only the wind in
the casuarinas
made a papery patter

when a cone spiralled
its way in front of
their steps

it was enough
to breathe them
apart

When I like what I write
it's as though my heart is melting on the page
thoughts open and close like night anemones
and the words perfume the empty air

Marking Time

I won't punish spring for starting up again
blame it for doing what it must do

it won't pain me to see wind rippling water
sun-dazzled bay   purpled cliff face

I won't resent the blue wren
the whispering birch

I can allow for the rustle of laughter
for those held with living arms

but there is one thing it's hard
to agree to

that I've lost any gratitude for…
find too generous…

…this privilege of
presence

there is no longer any point
in being here without you

I savour the two black birds
on morning grass
like our first coffee
in two tiny white cups

Sunday

we crept into candles
and chanting

I font-watered your
forehead with a cross

and kissed quiet your
wondering giggle

at the altar you reached
for the blessing hand

and held tight the fingers
of the surprised old priest

walking back
you asked if

tomorrow we could take
him breakfast

he looks so hungry
you worried

We had another
conversation today

the scorching wind that had
withered us for years

blew us hard and pure
into moonstones

our voices mere
and simple opals

beauties of change

Down poured the rain
closed windows steamed
with cold tears

summer and children
scattered
like wet falling leaves

time now
for woman's
potted tea

I have begun to store your love
like plants store starch
larders fill with food

I'm piling it up in buckets
for those days
lost at sea

The moon looked
glum on the
grey   wet sand

left over from
a night of tossing
and calling

what others are
spent and splattered
this new day dawning

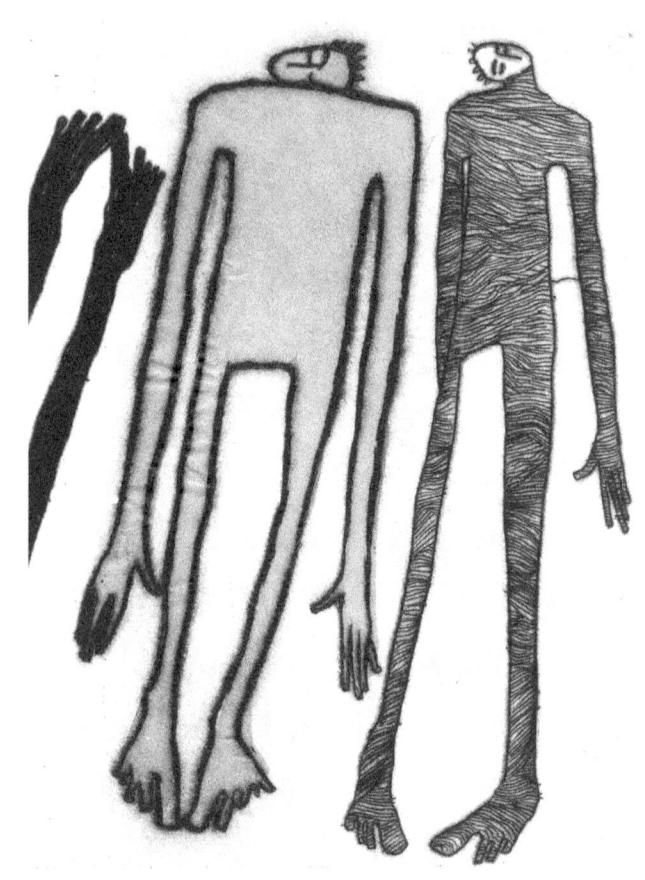

Reconcile

apologies   forgiveness
promises   belief
words about
difference   difficulty
bigness   oneness
what about sameness

As I become an old mother

transformation is no more
awesome than all the other
times of change
quickening of blood   breasts
belly

perhaps not so sudden
this forgetfulness
open-heartedness
don't mind ness
let it be ness

no more scruples   self criticism
no more separating
us from others
the eagle doesn't find fault
the bear doubt its rightness

crow
crocodile
killer whale
live gladly
without reservation

blue flower   black wave
broken red sky

the world is at its utmost
if you don't mind a little
dying

Treasure

daughters and mother
on retreat

gift of
woman's knowing

Meditation

by the lake
I poured
myself out

like fluid
over stem
and blossom

face of waxen peace
on green mat

water lily

Age has brought an urgency
I need to abstract   reduce   refine
what it is that I know and love
and pass it on

catch words that pluck
at the essence
and cradle that kindly

make an offering of noticing
wrapped in hope and gratitude

Elizabeth Goodsir

It was a fortunate thing that mum arrived
when I was emptying my studio
Decisive and unsentimental I had made
piles of etchings to throw out
I am grateful now that she rescued them

No longer making art I have a very different
perspective on my work

I can see each drawing for what it was…
a brief moment of mark making,
a conversation between my heart and hand
a spilling of my abstract thoughts

I no longer
need to be the critic
but can appreciate the
line-drawn story

Now these lines beside my mother's
written words have become a stitching
of a truly precious bundle

Madeleine Goodwolf

www.ingramcontent.com/pod-product-compliance
Lightning Source LLC
Chambersburg PA
CBHW062200100526
44589CB00014B/1879